Where Are We Now

Daniel Colegate

Where Are We Now
Dan Colegate

Copyright © 2019 Dan Colegate

All rights reserved.

If you enjoy this book, please leave a review.

Thank you for your support

Find out more at

www.estheranddan.com

www.facebook.com/estheranddan

www.instagram.com/estheranddan

For Esther

Thank you for seeing beyond my stories

Contents

Introduction...1

A Little Note On Reading These Poems.....................3

An Ant With The Truth On Its Back...........................5

Dying Game 6

Fence 7

Must do this, must do that.......................................8

The Time Of Civilisation 10

Lady Time..12

Going 13

Dying Seconds...14

Facebook Graveyard...15

Semi-coffin..16

Ride Of Life 17

Be Still 18

Bonfire 19

Distraction 20

Easy 21

Glory 22

Freedom 23

Hello Change..24

A Bee In The Wind 25

Flatline Man...26

Kindness...28

Equilibrium 29

Environment Song 30

Bang 32

Quantum...33

Seedling 34

Nature's Daydream 35

Pettyness 37

The Voices 38

Language 39

Equal 40

Ripples 41

Ripples – Part 2 42

Anxious Dawn 43

Nuclear 44

Friction 45

Oxford Dreams 47

Stillness 48

Tuesday 49

Quiet Despair 50

Seeking 51

Possessions 53

Preacher 55

Journal 56

Perspective 57

The Odd One Out 58

Ocean of demand 59

Hurricane 60

The Art Of Forgetting 61

Thank You 62

Acknowledgements 63

Also By The Author 64

Introduction

I've always loved words and stories, although it took me a very long time to realise just how powerful and important they are.

My love affair with stories began when I was very young. As a child I read a lot, usually at night. I'd lie face down on the edge of my bed with my bedroom door propped open while holding a book open on the floor so that I could read by the light from the hallway. That way, if mum or dad happened to go to the bathroom I could easily roll back into bed and pretend to be asleep instead of reading yet another book at 4 a.m on a school night. It was during these quiet, private, most-treasured moments that I first heard White Fang howl, charged into Mordor with Frodo and saw Poirot twirl his moustaches. Even back then I saw getting lost in a good story as my way of melting into happiness.

Yet I never saw my reading life as part of 'real' life, and I certainly didn't consider my reading as being anything more than entertainment. The world around me seemed to allow a certain amount of fun and escapism, but only once the serious stuff was taken care of, which is probably why I'd try and steal so much extra reading time by staying up all night with my books.

Roll forward into adulthood and I was a scientist and I was a sportsman. I had a first-class Oxbridge chemistry degree, a PhD and an academic job. At weekends I would wear lycra and make my legs hurt from the saddle of my road bike, periodically entering races which hurt even more. I still read books, although they felt more like a guilty pleasure, wasting time I could be spending doing something useful.

A few more years later I nearly died. That's the short version of course, although it is arguably the most important detail. A few months after that my wonderful partner, Esther, and I drove away from our suburban life, our jobs and (we hoped) our worries in a second-hand motorhome. We told our friends we'd be back in a year but we secretly hoped it would be longer. That was five years ago now and we are still leading a nomadic life.

Living a life removed from so many of the structures we'd grown up to consider normal, even essential, has taught us many things. For example, it's shown us how few material things we need to be genuinely happy, and that having fewer possessions is even part of happiness for us. It's compelled us to take a crash course in how we communicate with each other. It's proved that even when circumstances seem frightening and bleak, that what we need the most might be just an instant away. And it's shown us that, ultimately, we can never really run away from our worries because they are contained within the stories we carry in our heads. We can distract ourselves, lie to ourselves, even numb ourselves out, but in the end we have to face them.

As part of that process, of facing up to my worries, I decided to write down my life story. I suppose I thought it was an interesting story in itself, but then again, I was biased. What I didn't expect when I started writing 'my story' was that I would discover and strip away so many of my own, previously unquestioned, beliefs about myself. About who I was and why I was that way. Yes, I grew up with an embarrassing health condition. Yes, I'd played a lot of highly competitive sports. No, my family didn't really 'do' feelings and emotions. But so what? My story went through various rewrites as I struggled to work out which of these jumbled and often conflicting perspectives I was trying to share when it finally dawned on me. They were all just stories, and that the me beneath those stories was so much more than any of them. That's when I finally realised how powerful words and the stories that we build with them really are, especially the stories we believe about ourselves.

It's also when I started writing poetry.

Dan Colegate – 2019

2

A Little Note On Reading These Poems

I don't want to tell you how to read a poem. Probably you already know and besides, poems are personal, not only for the person who writes them but also for the person reading them. However you read, whatever your internal rhythm is and whatever a poem stirs in you is for you to experience. There is no right or wrong way to read a poem.

That said, if you can and would like to, I'd encourage you try and read my poems out loud. Many of them were written by me speaking the words out loud and feeling for what came next. Or, if it's not appropriate to read out loud or you just don't want to, read them in your head as though you were saying them out loud. You don't have to pretend to be on stage, just read them simply, slowly and peacefully and try and follow the punctuation instead of the lines.

Read them in the garden, in the bath, or on the loo if you like. Or if you're really brave (unlike me) read them out loud on the train on your way to work (if you do this, please ask someone to film it and send me a copy).

Then, when you finish reading a poem, I'd suggest taking a moment to be still so you can try and get in touch with what you're feeling. Do you feel happy? Sad? Awkward? Do you feel a mixture? Where in your body do you feel it? Or do you feel nothing at all? Whatever it is, take a moment to just experience that feeling of happiness, sadness, awkwardness, nothingness or 'whateverness' you feel, then, when you're ready, take a breath.

Poetry isn't magic, the magic is inside you. All poetry can do is help you get in touch with it.

Happy Feeling

An Ant With The Truth On Its Back

I saw an ant with the Truth on its back,
it was tiny, and fickle, and if you don't have the knack
of following close he'll be lost in the crowd,
where the ants with their lies drown out the sound
of the Truth, pure yet feeble, what treasure he holds,
that pure-hearted lamb surrounded by wolves.
He totters and teeters, he slips and moves on,
he's carried that Truth all the places he's gone.
No other ant wants it and he can't put it down,
he can only keep moving, look sadly around
at his kin, so delighted with their colourful lies,
they can't see his beauty with their misguided eyes,
they think it's a lie that he carries along,
that their lie is the Truth, all others are wrong.
So billions of ants march around in their faith
that they're the only sane ant in this entire place,
and they bask in that sanity, they push others away,
they marvel at their brilliance, they want it all their way.
Hence the wrestling and tumult, the fighting uncouth
as billions of lies declare themselves Truth.
"You're mad!" - "No not me, can't you see you're insane?"
"What crazy disease exists in your brain?"
But the Truth-ant stays silent, no need to make war,
he carries the Truth and he knows what it's for.
For the Truth, plain and simple, tiny, even bland,
can hold all those lies in the palm of its hand
and Love them, unconditional, even as they resist,
for Love is the Truth, it's all that there is.

Dying Game

Faint ridges mark forgotten crests
of gently probing swells of sea,
while I sit here to do my best
to wonder what you want of me?
Sand grooves and falls beneath my toes
in endless patterns that cannot stay,
as one arises, another goes
and I question if that's just the way
that we mere grains must grist our days,
laying bricks to move for those to come,
or drifting in a sullen haze
knowing all we do will be undone.
So why then are we here at all?
A chance, a quirk of chemistry?
Do we rise up simply just to fall
and in between name ourselves free?
Or, if there's more, could it be true
that you're really me and I am you?
And those, and them, the many, the few,
all the sentience on this globe of blue?
In which case I undo myself
when I come next to make my mark,
and watch myself as failing health
carries me down into the dark.
Mortal and eternal both.
I die, I live, I go, I stay.
I'm buried and I raise a toast
to the undone things I do this day.

Fence

I put up a fence and I stood on both sides,
on one master the other a slave,
that eternal conundrum, that endless divide,
which one did I build it to save?
For both are within me, I rule, I obey,
I do as I'm told and I tell,
and I find uses for both so I really can't say
which one's heaven and which is one is hell?
To be required to know, to state and command
how it is that this life should unfold,
then worry about whether all my demands
will be delivered in the way they were told.
Or submit to fate and release all my dreams
to the whims of a world I can't know,
while freeing my mind beyond all that it seems
that this life is willing to show.
Should I drift or decree? Should I fight or give way?
On which side of the fence will I find
that magnificent joy at the end of each day
when the fence is all in my mind?

Must do this, must do that

Must do this, must do that,
go to the gym or I'll get fat,
walk the dog, poop-scoop the lawn,
three jobs done, it's barely dawn.
Miss the bus, now must rush,
charge the high street, fight the crush,
at my desk, a minute to spare,
working hard, boss don't care.
Morning bagels and pastry buns,
thank God I went to 'Bums-n-tums'.
Watch the clock, soon be lunch,
could I leave now and call it brunch?
Thankfully boss has a so-called meeting,
look outside, it's his wife he's greeting.
Down the street, there he goes,
time to take a trip to Tesco's.
Fill my basket from healthy shelves
plus a sweet or three to treat myself.
Back at my desk at caffeine o'clock,
start to nod off, get a shock,
client calls, I've missed a conference,
like I care, their product's nonsense.
Hour late, traffic for miles,
arrive to a room of frosty smiles,
try to care, a waste of time,
wish I could say what's on my mind.
"Is that a wig or a bad comb-over?"
Mustn't laugh, keep my composure.
Leave at four, desk or home?
Great, the boss is on the phone.
"Get back here A. S. A. P."
"The M.D. just popped in for tea!"
Get back just as the M.D leaves,
he and boss seem thick as thieves.
Something's up? More cuts and sackings?
If so, I doubt I'll get their backing.

M.D. gone, I'm out the door,
can't stand the place a moment more.
Kids to fetch and clubs to do,
swimming, archery and baseball too.
Home at eight, ready meals
bubble in the microwave, know how it feels
getting zapped by invisible forces,
like a kick in the balls by ten race horses.
Baths and squabbles, pyjama wars
end with loudly slamming doors.
Wine o'clock, best make it two,
other half gets home, "Let's have a few."
Asleep on our chests by half past ten,
seven hours, do it all again.

The Time Of Civilisation

The boiling sun scorched the Earth until
the sand grains themselves grew afraid.
The Civilised Man, stranded and abandoned
in a sea of dust looked skywards bewildered.

On the horizon appeared a speck,
a speck which became a shimmer,
a shimmer which grew limbs and birthed
a man. A squat man with skin of leather
and a face like a raisin.

Slow and surefooted, the man of leather
approached the Civilised Man.
"Ah, a savage" thought the Civilised Man,
"to be sure he will save me with his wily ways."

The Savage came within earshot
and Civilised fired the first volley.
"What time is it?" Civilised demanded of the Savage,
adding, "my watch is broken," by way of explanation.

"Time?" responded the Savage,
 "I do not understand your question."

"I know many things."
"I know the beasts of the air and the land
and the places they must rest."
"I know the veins of water which infuse the sand
and provide the lifeblood of my people."
"I know the ways of the Spirits who watch over us every moment,
even as we speak now."
"I know when to plant the seeds and when to harvest them."
"I know when the wild berries are lush and ripe."
"I know when to rise and when to sleep."
"I know when to make love to my wife...."
"....and when not to!" he added, smiling.

"But I do not know this Time?"

"My gosh! How can you live without knowing the time?" responded Civilised.
"After you take me home, I shall send you a watch as a reward."

Lady Time

I feel her touch. She has no hands.
Her icy breath. She has no lungs.
Her incessant gaze. She has no eyes.
Her appetite. She takes the Young.

And in their place leaves husks and shells
who, to compensate, we label wise.
But without youth they barely stir,
we park them up until they die.

But we, the ageless ones, go on,
watching others her touchless touch befall,
never knowing she feasts upon us too
until, too late, we hear her call.

Going

I didn't ask to be here, but now I choose to stay,
yet despite this choice I yet still fear I'll have to go away.
I know not where I'm going and I know not when I'll go,
so there seems little point in crying, perhaps it's better not to know.

Dying Seconds

I've scaled many mountains,
I've bridged many streams,
I've cycled many passes,
I've followed all my dreams.
Yet when I reached the rainbow
and touched her glittering end,
I saw her false illusion
but had no more time to spend.
A few remaining hours
were all I had in hand,
with no treasure to reward me
for my adventures in this land.
Wearily I trudged back
to the place that had been home,
a place long since forgotten
since I'd first set out to roam.
Yet what did I discover
in that long-departed place
but the treasures I'd sought after
in the arms of Love's embrace.
My family beheld me,
they took me in their arms,
and with my few remaining minutes
they washed away all harms,
forgave me all my absence,
gently held my many flaws,
where I'd expected to find barriers
were only open doors.
I've lived a full life certain,
climbing countless hills and trees,
but my most fulfilling seconds
were unquestionably these.

Facebook Graveyard

When gravestones are dead will we Facebook instead
the memorials to our lives?
Erecting digital pillars containing colourful thrillers
of how we mortally thrived?
So that family may, if they choose to stay,
shed beautifully virtual tears
over vast lines of code where nobody knows
if it's a testament to our years,
or simply fake news, extremist new views,
to taint what once we became,
or rewritten stuff to replace the old guff
that moderators labelled too tame.
And as lost friends hit share to show that they care
they're browsing for a brand-new TV,
for the old one's too small, only just half a wall,
how can they be expected to see
the likes and new mentions which hold their attention
as your remnants grow cold in their urn,
while your digital self remains on a shelf
awaiting deletion in turn.

Semi-coffin

Sealed in my semi-coffin life
by the tumult and chaos pressing in,
my dreams die in my self-sought strife
as day by day my life is thinned,
until, my childish dreams all dead,
my long-held cherished means of coping,
I face myself inside my head
unadorned by future hoping.
And so encloses the crushing dark,
the grip the world taught me to fear,
my days stretch on without a spark
as I cling to the past, all I hold dear.
Yet my glory days are withered and lost,
so much expected, so little achieved.
All that's left are pale ghosts
upon whose shrine I bend and grieve.
But as my body racks with shame
at all I dreamed but left undone,
I find despair begins to wane,
replaced by a new rising sun.
A sun of acceptance within my soul
now freed from life's strait-jacket aims,
released from chasing receding goals,
emancipation from the pain
as slowly I learn to simply be,
that whatever arises will be enough.
It took me a life of angst to see
right through this angry world of bluff.

Ride Of Life

The ride of life is turning
and we've chosen to hop on,
with no clue how long we'll ride for
since one day we'll all be gone.
But for this vanishing passage
on our unknown count of spins,
we still get to make choices
on some most important things.

Do we wave our hands and cheer
or do we sit back crouched in fear?
Do we help others approaching
or ask them not to sit too near?
Some say the ride has no meaning,
that it's a pointless cosmic aside,
but to love with heart and feeling,
I think that's why we ride.

Be Still

The pine tree neither loathes the chill nor longs for the warmth of dawn.
But she enjoys it.

The mountain doesn't dream of snow nor count the days of summer.
They both delight him.

The stream cannot imagine the sea or rush to complete her bends.
She experiences them.

And the moon has no preference whether she waxes or wanes.
It's all beautiful to her.

Why then do I spend my days comparing? Hot and cold? Tall and small? Far or near?
Which do I prefer today? It will only change tomorrow.
Be still.
Be still.

Be.
Still.

Do you hear it now?

Bonfire

In desperation I built a bonfire of all my worldly ambitions
only to find my True Self glowing hot and vibrant among the ashes.
It had always been there, buried by my material dreams,
but only when I stripped myself of what I'd convinced myself I was
could I see clearly what I've always been.

Distraction

I went to the beach to ponder
but instead aimlessly wandered
for miles of distraction
with a pleasing sense of action
bought on by the walking
while in my head much talking
with imaginary people,
who were passing through my mind.

I said hello to Newton
who wanted to borrow my futon
and gave advice to Gandhi
who was feeling rather randy
which upset Marie Curie
and put her in a fury
until away they drifted,
or at least fell behind.

So I turned back to my issue
with the resolve of a wet tissue
which lasted just a second
until more distraction beckoned
such as shells and wheeling seagulls
which was enough to leave my mind full
for many more long moments,
as I stayed happily blind.

To the reason that I came here
to confront that nagging deep fear
that my life is whistling by me
at a pace completely barmy
and that if there is a purpose
then it's hid beneath a surface
which I'm too scared to look under,
in case of what I find.

Easy

Ups and downs, lefts and rights,
lower lows, higher heights.
No-one said it would be easy.

Deeper silence, louder fights,
lighter days, darker nights.
No-one said it would be easy.

Possibly, maybe, should-be, might,
worrying wrongs, uplifting rights.
No-one said it would be easy.

The fall, the letting go, the frights.
An opportunity for growth ignites.
But still, no-one said it would be easy.

And loving guidance infinite
lights the way for deep insight.
Perhaps it never will be easy?

With courage follow your inner light.
Release all that you once held tight.
It no longer matters if it's easy.

Time to help the world unite.
Pure love and joy will all excite.
And in graceful flow, find your easy.

Glory

The glory of this moment,
the wind, the smoke, the noise,
is worth more than all the trinkets
in this life of plastic toys,
which can titillate a fancy,
or answer to the call
of material libido
behind cerebral walls,
while the real burns in fire,
crumbling to flaming brands
which could be rescued in a second
if we'd just hold out our hands,
across the widest little nothing
filled up with our disgrace,
separating reality and perception,
the divide we dare not face.

Freedom

Dance me, squeeze me, twist me, peel me,
release me from all I would be,
within you, without you, beside you, among you,
my God how I wish to be free
of all that we shake, that we make, that we break, that we
forge if only to see,
just what it is that they burn, that they tear, that they spurn, that they
remove from our life-bestowed glee...

...while we let them.

Hello Change

Oh great, it's you, demanding change,
my first reaction to shut the door,
to close out what you're here to bring,
I simply can't handle any more.
Why can't you just go and leave me be?
You've called too many times before!
The last thing that I need right now
is more challenges, of that I'm sure.
I know you claim it's good for me
but you leave me crying on the floor.
You say it's the only way to grow
but I just can't face another war
of ego and soul, of heart and mind,
as I fight in the mire of my own manure.
Last time you promised one more push
but your promise turned out premature.
Oh yes, you're tempting, I'll give you that.
Offering peace and light to me to lure
me forward to a better way
to face my demons, to become my cure.
Still, I'm frightened, I'm holding back
from this gift you dangle that remains obscure,
though I know deep down that I believe
you can bring me safe towards the shore.
Okay, I'll do it, I'll take your hand,
let's walk together, though insecure.
I'll trust in you this one more time
as we tread towards a life more pure,
where the earthquakes of fate will not erode
our tranquillity which will endure.
I'm sorry I tried to shut you out,
when change is what this life is for.

A Bee In The Wind

If nectar is Love and I am the bee
then what is this wind which roars through the trees?
It buffets and shreds my feather-lite wings
with bills, jobs and deadlines, such unforgiving things.
I leave every morning with one aim in mind,
to gather up all the Love I can find
but almost as soon as I launch at the start
this mighty tornado encircles my heart.
It blinds, gags and chokes up my will to succeed,
it clogs up my passion, I can no longer feed
in the arms of this tyrant who throws me about,
I may as well yield, have not even gone out.
But just when I fear I can no longer go on
my Love whispers a lesson, an urge to stay strong.
This tormenting storm arises from me,
I need only release it and I can fly free.
The terrors remain but I need no longer fear
their trivial demands, I'm always right here
in the heart of the moment, invincible soul,
being still within the whirlwind, that is my goal.

Flatline Man

For thirty flatline years I learned
to feel nought and call it good,
and if ever a supressed flicker yearned
to be heard, it was misunderstood.

With each wasted year my layers grew,
protection against my self-seen flaws,
and though approaches were made by some
I shut my windows, closed my doors.

Until, concrete-covered from without
with a lifestyle to match in diploma beige,
I seemed impermeable to all no doubt,
except you whom I could not dissuade.

I began to mimic that trait of love
to play my part as a loyal man,
But fear gripped me in her vicelike glove
and away again I turned and ran.

Still you tried, I fled, you wept,
I returned and made you weep some more,
I know not where our flame was kept
and I'm not sure that you did for sure.

I supposed you hoped that time's soft blows
would yield me up as the man you saw,
beneath the shell, another show,
a feeling, happy, hidden core.

But time was failing, failing fast,
as external blows strengthened my resolve
to remain subdued and make it last,
until death took me to His fold.

Then something gentler than before,

erroneous, an inner blow,
and from that first followed many more,
igniting a seedling desire to grow.

Familiar shells are hard to shed,
lifelong ones yet harder still,
but finding my inner self not dead
each twinge of pain was matched with thrill.

You stayed the course, you held my hand,
soothed me as shed my skin,
at times it bled like grating sand
as each layer shrunk to tissue thin.

Anger and rage were first to die,
guilt and shame then followed suit,
'til happiness was heard to cry
and love, not fakery, took root.

Oh joyous, ecstatic, emotional dawn,
the sun that rises on the sea,
I feel it now, no longer a pawn
to our flatline culture's trickery.

Kindness

Equilibrium

To be at equilibrium
with all around the same,
no contrast, change or difference,
must be a most dull frame.

A picture of all greyness,
a single-coloured scene,
compared to light and darkness
what could that even mean?

Because without pain, where's pleasure?
Without night, where's day?
Without hurt, where's love gone?
Without boredom, play?

So I'm grateful for the chaos,
the ups, downs, lefts and rights,
I'll accept majestic daytime
be recognised through knowing night.

Environment Song

Rise up, rise up, the crisis has called,
No way, I've got work, I could never do that,
Sleep-walking for decades, ignoring it all,
I refuse to believe it, it can't be that bad,
Air and water polluted, the soil is dry,
I know it's a problem but there won't be a war,
The moment you see it, it's hard not to cry,
I already recycle, I don't have time to do more,
Turn away from your office, be part of the change,
They should just get a job, that's what they should do,
If your refusing to see it you must be deranged,
They're just middle-class hippies who can't see what's true,
With football and pies at the top of your list,
Puffed up with degrees worth the rags in my car,
Or worrying about the telly you've missed,
It's all 'Jolly Good Tarquin, let's go to the bar',
Just a gammon-faced oaf with your rag Daily Mail,
To get stoned on their lattes and misguided beliefs,
Refusing to accept your system has failed,
Never a real day's work, they're completely naïve,
That your children will pay for your decades of greed,
With their pashminas and gap years and crocodile tears,
It's your fault, admit it, you planted these seeds,
For the dregs of society and minority fears,
When you chose to believe the hate and the lies,
Blockading the highways and underground routes,
Of self-serving leaders who had you take sides,
Wearing faux 'ethnic' outfits that cost more than my suit,
Against anyone different, anyone new,
Why should I give up the few pleasures of my day,
Anyone at all who seemed different to you,
For their nagging agendas and elitist word play,
Now you're stuck in the past, you gullible fools,
Degrading the truth for which our ancestors died
Lashing out in your meanness, so stupidly cruel,
We're grown-ups, we'll manage, take it all in our stride,

But it can't change the fact that your ways are now dead,
So shove all your placards where the sun doesn't shine,
As we undo your mistakes and build a new world instead.
Do what you want with your life, you're not changing mine.

When the truth falls between two voices of hate,
then the argument stalls until perhaps it's too late.

Bang

Out of nothing, something,
the auditors would weep,
yet not-quite-nothing birthing
a something woke from sleep,
when everything exploded,
exploded in a sea
of unadulterated one-thing,
a one-thing that would be
everything's container,
the nothing beyond the walls,
but is nothing really something?
We just don't know at all.

Quantum

A contract sealed before time began,
before nothing exploded
and quantum raged.
Ages advanced, energy merged,
coalescing into planets, galaxies and stars
until volcanoes cooled into mountains.
Ages more, man came forth.
Blinking, standing, advancing and learning.
Civilisation creeping.
Millenia later, there we were,
a pink scarf and a threadbare cap
glancing and wondering at something.
Waves of joy, crashes of pain,
marking years with lessons unseen.
Losing, drowning in labels
until the times were ripe
for the chrysalis of conditioning to split.
New forms of being emerged.
But not new, timeless.
Your self and my self.
Tentatively realising our being.
And so it was that we became
our eternal contract.
Actions. Events. Unfolding.
All leading towards this moment.
Then this one.
Now this.
Thank you.

Seedling

Even nothing isn't nothing,
it's quantum don't you know?
Full of fleeting fluctuations
at least one of which did blow
into the bang of our beginning,
our existential starter's gun,
setting sudden space expanding
while nascent gravity formed suns,
which one day went supernova,
creating the building blocks of you.
That's right, you're made of stardust,
it sounds foolish but it's true.
Which means every quark inside you
was once enmeshed with me,
and her, and him, and them and those,
every single thing you see
emerged from the self-same seedling
just a short, deep-time ago,
which is a powerful truth to cling to
in this life's unceasing flow.

Nature's Daydream

In the palm of nature I found a man,
a restless, wandering mirror-man
and I found he looked like me.
He'd made a shelter beside a stream
and lay down smiling as though he dreamed
in a manner wholly free,
while diamond eyes gazed to the sky
enchanted to watch the swallows fly
from sea to sparkling sea.

Silently, I stood a while,
fascinated by this earthly child
whose features were my own,
and yet not me
as I could see
for all was overgrown.

A longing overtook me then,
a yearning for the lost time when
I could have been that man,
before all the years filled my heart with tears
and replaced all of my dreams with fears
to make sure that I ran,
away from all my primal lusts
and drove me to do all I must
to become material man.

And as longing turned into despair
my other life looked up with care
to hold out his work-worn hand,
which was filled with seeds
for all I'd need
to join him on the sand.
And as I drew near
the lesson grew clear,
this one was up to me.

The seeds were mine, so was the sadness,
I'd chosen before but chosen madness
and learned to call sorrow glee,
but if I planted these simple seeds,
hoed my garden, cut back the weeds,
I could yet still be free.

The clarity swept me off my feet
to dump me back on a clanging street
where a new choice was my own.
Would I still lay blame on this worldly game
for the disappointments I became,
or embody what I'd been shown?
And plant those seeds for all I'd need
to live a life totally freed
in rapture with the joy I'd grown.

Pettyness

No-one seems to know me,
least of all myself,
so I stand upon a pedestal
to push you off your shelf.
For I found I could go no higher
to rise above your head,
so I decided it was easier
to take you down instead.

The Voices

"Of course you can do it" they told me,
and I could, so all was fine,
but the next time, when I couldn't,
they said the fault was all mine.
"Did you try your best?" they questioned,
"I gave it all that I had" I replied,
but expectation outmatched reason
so they told me that I'd lied.
That all I'd shown was my weakness,
cowardice, to their very great shame.
How dare I put forth such a performance?
A performance performed in their name.
Yet even then they still insisted
it wasn't my failure which hurt them the most,
but the fact I'd resorted to lying,
that I'd faced them with outlandish boasts
that I'd given it all that I could have,
a claim that was clearly not true.
So why could I not have just owned them,
my colours of cowardly hue?
And as the critical voices grew louder,
dashing the confidence I'd once entertained,
pretty soon my defences had fallen,
mute agreement was all that remained.
So, perhaps they were right in their charges,
that I surrender before having my say,
when I can't even summon the resistance
of standing and walking away.
Though I swear that I would if I could have,
I swear that I've tried and I've tried,
but the voices have infinite power
when it's your mind their living inside.

Language

It's matter cry the physicists, which is also energy.
It's God and all his Prophets, claims Deuteronomy.
It's pure spirits says the New Age, within which we're all free.
It's loving chant the Buddhists, which gives us reason to be.
So many names and labels, jumbled confusingly,
but they're all speaking of the same Truth, metaphorically.
That if you see your sister struggling and you hold her caringly,
then you transcend all of the language and help the world to see
that divisions are illusions, so unnecessary,
when beneath our decorations we're the same, you and me.

Equal

I don't fear death, I do fear pain,
I don't mind weather, I do mind rain,
I don't want money, I do want food,
I don't get angry, I can be rude
if you spit upon me as you pass me by,
think you're above me, I wonder why?
Since once I was you, a smiling suit,
bedecked in glitter, my smile so cute
to charm from pockets the finest gold,
yet now I've fallen I've found my soul.
I can see things clearly, my mind stripped bare,
like your armour is bullshit, your cash doesn't care
to whom it belongs, in whose nameless account
it sits in small piles or one obscene amount.
But by all means take safety, indeed be my guest,
hoard all of your trappings, be just like the rest,
because when you sit beside me, and one day you will,
one way or another I'll bear no ill will.
I'll share all the little that I still call my own
and together we'll wait 'til it's time to go home.
Equal we all are, we all want the same.
Love, food, warmth and shelter, the rest's just a game.

Ripples

Our ripples slip into the void
to do their work, we're blind
to see the places that they reach,
the beings that they find,
their gentle touch caressing,
inspiring and changing minds,
with the power to reach anger,
uncoil it and unwind
as they steer new hearts to loving
and move them to be kind,
so as you wake each morning
to a face a blank page unlined,
remember to tread softly
for the ripples you leave behind.

Ripples – Part 2

Don't dismiss the ripples you create

Anxious Dawn

An anxious dawn arrives unwelcome.
The slumberers are dragged from dreamland
to question what this day is for?

They've asked the question these thousand days
and will continue to ask until
the answer they receive tastes good.

Like sugared caffeine in a hearty mug,
layers of jam on crisp, toasted bread,
and a juicy biscuit, fresh-dunked and melting.

Pleasure. Pleasure is easy to find,
running down in myriad inexpensive forms
to titillate, delight and distract.

But happiness, happiness eludes them,
these pampered, lucky, drifting slumberers
who arise each day asking why.

Why is happiness asked of me?
That most elusive gift, the grail.
I have all the stars except the one you ask for.

And so another day passes,
comatose in excruciating pleasure,
full knowing tomorrow will dawn unfulfilled.

Nuclear

I see your pain, I see your power,
as it closes and opens like a delicate flower,
encasing your furnace-fire within,
there's so much hidden beneath your skin,
waiting to burst into the sky
and glow forever in lights which fly
as flickering, surging, strands of love
which rain their joy from high above,
to absorb the vengeance infecting man
by spreading peace as only you can.
So never hide your magic heart,
its secret ways are works of art.
You have a purpose, never doubt,
your nuclear fire can't go out.

Friction

Our biggest addiction is attachment to friction,
like our minds can't settle in bliss,
though we'll seek out new pleasure in planned blocks of leisure,
in time, it feels amiss.
As when joy lasts too long it starts to feel wrong,
something we can't justify,
in this world of fast action and stressful distraction,
so instead, we find reasons to cry.
As when the world sees that we're down on our knees
then someone may reach out their hand,
to console us in grief, a blessed relief,
from our lives of self-conscious demands.
And it's how we bond too when we're all feeling blue,
bemoaning this world of full of wrongs,
and why not indeed, it's a basic human need
to feel as though we belong.
Which is easier for sure when we paint ourselves poor
and hide all our brilliance away,
until eventually we just don't want to see
the magnificence of life every day.
Because we're scared of our essence, our beating strong presence,
the infinite power we hold,
to spread light, love and peace until all conflicts cease,
it's true, but it's not what we're told.
Instead we tell ourselves tales of the reasons we fail
to create the lives in our hearts,
and blame it on others, like fathers and mothers,
for giving us imperfect starts.
But imagine instead if we got out of our heads
and shone like the stars we could be,
creating a world with our brilliance unfurled
and every sentient being felt free
to look on a stranger with no sense of danger,
just the pure light of love in their soul,
where we'd smile as we talk and dance as we walk
with global joy our primary goal.

So put down your pain, there's nothing to gain
from carrying it one step more,
you're amazing, it's true, there's no-one like you,
so own it, it's what you're here for.

Oxford Dreams

From 'ayup me duck, don't give a fuck'
to dreaming spires and Oxford luck.
Risen on connected wings
to lofty goals and great good things
with a life more suited to glitterati
not one who found wild daisies 'arty',
and no time for shite and boring crap
like Raphael, Mozart and Bach.
Just aptitude and blunt finesse,
determined to win life's aimless quest,
but can the win be worth the cost
if the price is that the self is lost?
The origin severed, the bosom forlorn,
no yearning of a loss to mourn?
Just another layer of false façade,
a masquerade, a shade, a card,
over-played and ever shallow,
a fertile soul abandoned fallow
in pursuit of life's material gains,
a stampede of like-minded brains
charging mindless, stocks and shares,
bulls madder than the mad march hares.
Not love, oh no, that weak soft chink,
that hindrance, that vulnerable blink
when facing a terrifying world alone,
then suddenly, the time's all flown.
No chance he's gone, cannot be saved,
Alone he goes to his lonely grave.

Stillness

I tried to sit still today.

I failed.

I was, of course, victorious in a purely physical sense.

My lungs breathed, my eyelids flickered, and a trillion chemical reactions progressed undisturbed, but, in a superficial way at least I was 'still'.

My limbs were obediently motionless.

Not so my mind.

I planned.

I spoke with imaginary memories.

I felt claustrophobic, apathetic, panicked, worried and elated, in no particular order.

This all accounted for the first minute or so.

It went downhill after that.

Certainly, stillness is wonderful. A gift.

A goal that is worth aspiring to.

Personally, however, much of the time I consider stillness a proper bastard.

Tuesday

Today was the day I died.
For a handful of blissful, eternal, rampant seconds
I ceased to be.
Dead to Myself. Dead to the world. Dead.
And yet, still I breathed, breathing myself still.
Breathing myself into death.
Those breaths were all I was,
all I ever would be,
all I would ever need to be.
Those breaths were nothing,
they were the entire universe
caught within a dry-lipped whispering hiss.
I saw it then, fragile and perfect.
And then I lost it.
My shallow mortal breaths returned,
stealing up on me, carrying with them my vengeance,
my insecurity, my grasping nature,
the pathetic deals I make with myself.
I was alive. I was more dead than I ever knew.
Today was the day I died.
Today was Tuesday.

Quiet Despair

Oh sweet distraction, please, swallow me whole.
Devour my rage and vengeance.
Relish my frustration.
Carve up my imaginings and wash them down
with my rising bile.
Damn, this life is a merciless place
to be alone, accompanied by my ideas.
My dark self.
Chattering. Clammering. Chuntering.
Demanding satisfaction.
Fuck you! And fuck you too!
This silent friendless room is torture.
I am my inquisition.
But you, you can be my saviour.
Feed me, drink me, drug me.
Send a velvet breeze to soothe my restless ocean.
Oblivion, send your angels to relieve
this hell I have created and despise.
Only man could create self-loathing
and blame it on the world.

Seeking

As childhood victories fell away
I found myself quite lost,
beneath maturity, pressing down,
I discovered to my cost
that praise had not prepared me
for the failures I'd believe
would soon grow to define me,
to drive a growing need
to turn my seeking outward
to find answers to my pain,
to identify a reason
why my life seemed all in vain.
Why such promise had been promised
but such failure arrived.
Why, though I'd put my best foot forward,
I'd stumbled down and dived?
But then sweet relief did soothe me
from the pages of a book,
with a covering mandala
I knew with a single look
that herein lay salvation,
that I held within my hands,
the perfect map and compass
to negotiate the sands
of life's trapdoors beneath me,
and then another book arose,
with a message subtly different,
a new message that I chose.
And so began my learning,
my accumulation game,
jumping from one answer to another,
no two ever quite the same.
Though at their heart the message,
"let go, you are enough",
it wasn't that I wanted
so I skipped across the cuff

to the practices, the journals,
the audio, the guests,
the conferences, the workshops,
I sat them all like tests.
Each one with feel-good factor,
a new milestone achieved,
like a new-age monk in training
reforming all I'd once believed.
And yes, it was exciting
to be always moving on,
but, without knowing it could happen,
one day my self was gone,
lost amid the jungle
of the countless things I'd sought,
the lessons and the mantras
so passionately taught
from the sweet-shop of the soulful,
the inner wisdom crew,
repackaging the ancient
in colourful forms anew,
spinning my thoughts into a tumult,
pulled both this way and that,
I could no longer feel salvation
from the comfort of my mat,
just myriad hollow mantras
all jostling to be said,
a thousand peaceful passages
all trying to be read,
because instead of learning stillness
I'd simply re-filled the hole
of doubtfulness with seeking
when I'd tried to patch my soul.

Possessions

In pursuit of more possessions, most fashionable of obsessions,
we require expanding new homes,
where we pile the clutter from cellar to gutter
to admire from reclining thrones.
'Til one day we say we'll put it away,
so we take a trip to IKEA,
to wander the aisles perusing the styles
and filling our card with ideas.
Four flat-packs later and we've created a crater
in our previous mountain of stuff,
which we enjoy much at first but soon grow in our thirst
to fill it with ever more guff.
A new blender here, some new cycling gear,
and the mountains swiftly returns.
But with material gains like this to maintain,
it's a worry just how much we earn,
completing the threesome that curtails our freedom
of stuff and storage and cash,
where from each to the other we race one another
in a smiling competitive dash.
All caught in the prism of capitalism,
our doctrine from the day we arrive,
where happiness costs and success can be lost
in an instant if we fail to strive
for the Great God of Growth, like we've taken an oath
to bow down at His mighty throne,
for the promise of plenty 'til the bank account's empty,
in which case we take out a loan.
And though we know it's a greed for more stuff we don't need,
that the best things in life are all free,
this world makes us fear that all those we hold dear
will suffer if we heed our heart's plea
to sidestep the race, duck out of the chase,
and let our pursuit of more cease,
where we lower our stress by redefining success
and learning what it is to release

all the fear and the doubts that we're all missing out,
somehow, in a way we can't say,
seeking just a little more although we're never quite sure
more of 'what' at the end of the day?

Preacher

I preach and beseech from a pulpit of sand,
ever shifting beneath sinking-sore feet,
as I toss out advice from fear-shaking hands,
endorsing while I myself beat
against inner-heart walls, refusing to fall,
so do as I say and not as I do,
I'm just lost that's all, my life's in a stall,
but the advice part is made no less true.

Journal

I cast off all my shackles in a book beside my bed,
a journal some may call it, or a book of Truth instead,
where the issues in my tissues can be set upon a page
and so, at least in theory, release all of my rage,
and process all my sadness, my worries and my doubt,
just open up the floodgates and let it all pour out.
Until my head is empty and I'm free to apparently be
more fluid in the moment as a more me kind of me.
But the reality's quite different, or at least that's what I've found,
since I rather miss the shackles which held me to the ground.
'Cause if I put down all my stories, then who the hell am I?
And without all my issues then I have to question why
I'm existing in the first place, why am I even here?
It's a perfectly valid question but it fills me up with fear
as it's easier to blame a parent for the reason that I doubt,
and a long-forgotten teacher for the reason that I shout,
and so never face the power that I really hold inside,
the power beneath the stories, the power that I hide.

Perspective

I know I was born lucky,
I'm sure that I was not,
I look back on life with gladness,
Mostly, I regret my lot,
My parents were always working,
My parents were never there,
To give us all we needed,
I never felt their care,
In school they praised my effort,
My grades were never enough,
With teachers that encouraged,
For teachers who were tough,
So I followed a path of learning,
My choices were never my own,
It taught me how to spread my wings,
I was trapped in what I'd known,
I travelled and I prospered,
Stuck in my own dead-end,
Thanks to people I encountered,
lost touch with all my friends,
Filling all my years with laughter,
My years like silent songs,
I never needed all the answers,
I knew only what was wrong,
Even in the hard times,
Life was always hard to bear,
I did my best to smile,
I hardly even cared,
And now I find my years are fading,
I look forward only to death,
I'm grateful for the gifts I've had,
I care even less for time still left,
A positive outlook has been my mantra,
There's only one way to see life,
For a life well-lived in joy.
A struggle full of strife.

The Odd One Out

Sometimes people really need
someone to be the 'odd one out'

Ocean of demand

I set sail for satisfaction across the ocean of demand,
with an aim to seize the sunset and crush it in my hands
'til it yielded up its brilliance, entirely to me,
so I wouldn't have to share it and only I would be
infused with all its power, only so much to go around,
which would bring me satisfaction above the scraps I'd found
while walking in the darkness of a life without it all,
a life of sharp desire, drunk on the sirens' call
of the promise of fulfilment, just a possession or two away,
on the beach of cast-off burdens and never-ending play.
For I could see the smiles on the faces of the tanned
as they jangled all their trinkets on sun-lit golden sands,
which is where my compass took me, once I'd chosen to let go,
of the man I thought I used to be and all he used to know,
by setting aside my kindness to embrace the growing need
to exercise my lusting in a society of greed.
But it wasn't what I expected, when I reached that sunset shore,
as I stood in a crumbling theme park, empty, still wanting more.
And as I cast my eyes back across that sea I'd sailed
I could finally see the treasures in the land where once I'd failed
to appreciate the richness of the life I'd lived to share
what little I had with others when I remembered how to care.

Hurricane

Change met me like a hurricane,
unseen but for its wake,
with indiscriminate destruction
as the ground began to shake,
tearing open scars like tissue,
scars I'd tried to hide
so that the world might love me,
though I still felt them inside.
Until, naked and without pretence,
as the gale raged around
my resistant futile crying
was lost within the sound
of my dreams and hopes in tatters,
beating and beaten in the wind,
of this seeming callous monster
punishing unknown sins.
"Why me? Why now?" I begged him,
"I've made such detailed plans,"
plans now scattered like detritus
with the other dust and sand.
Yet still the storm it flayed me,
whipping heart and skin and bone
relentless hour after hour,
erasing everything I'd known.
And when the storm subsided
all that remained was an idea,
an idea of who I could be
finally released from the fear
of expectation and of longing,
those cobwebs of the minds,
which had for so long entangled
my eyes and kept me blind,
'til the storm destroyed my blinkers
to the beauty of the now,
and I saw I could live fully
without fully knowing how.

The Art Of Forgetting

Imagine a birth without cameras,
a wedding with no silver frame,
old age without crinkled dry albums,
would our memories still look the same
without the visual aids we call golden
to keep the art of forgetting forgot?
No moment a moment forever
without the whir of a faux shutter-shot.
Would the "I do's" be lost like dead echoes?
Our tears lost the instant they dry?
Would blankness canvas our futures
as we long for our lost days gone by?
Or might we instead start to savour
new flutterings charged with the thrill
of knowing one chance at the present
which, if lost, becomes 'never will'?
Will we embrace our true mortal nature?
Will we urge to wring out each pause?
Will visual aids become pale phantoms
to the sensations our bodies will store?
Will we relive each technicolour instant,
available whenever we call?
Will our bodies replay us our pleasures
once our souls are released to feel all?
Will we remember the art of forgetting,
living now while accepting now's gone,
seizing all of our moments like lifeblood
while trying to hold on to none.

Thank You

Hello wonderful reader and thank you for making it all the way to the end of *Where Are We Now.*

I know you could have picked any number of books to read, but you picked this one and for that I am extremely grateful.

I hope that it gave you everything you hoped it would, plus a little surprise or two as well.

It would be wonderful if you'd take a few seconds to leave a review on Amazon.

Also, if you can, it would be really nice if you could share this book with your friends and family by sharing it on Facebook, Twitter, your local telephone box or by any other means you enjoy.

Thank you and best wishes.

Dan Colegate
May 2019

www.estheranddan.com

www.facebook.com/estheranddan

www.instagram.com/estheranddan

Acknowledgements

The poems in this book were written during a period of time chock full of victories, catastrophes, smiles, tears, dog hair, floor-sweeping, grocery shopping, world events and weather, in addition to a few other things as well.

In short, life went on, meaning that while I accept responsibility for any and all errors in this book (unless you liked any errors you found, in which I shall take the credit), the mere fact this book exists at all is thanks to the unwavering support of one particular person.

Esther, thank you, I love you.

Moo x

Dan Colegate – May 2019

Turn over for more by the author

Also By The Author

Love, Fluff & Chasing Butterflies
Dog Poems Inspired By An Amazing True Story

Love, Fluff & Chasing Butterflies is a glorious celebration of an amazing true story that underlines the special bond which can exist between dogs and their humans.

It was while touring through Europe in a motorhome that Dan & Esther decided to adopt Leela, an abandoned dog on the south coast of Spain. It wasn't something they'd ever planned to do, however, when she wagged her way towards them in a Spanish cafe they found themselves unexpectedly opening their rolling home to this cute little dog in need.

What they never expected was that just two weeks later Leela would give birth to six puppies! What came next was a story of love triumphing over circumstances as they turned their lives upside down to care for the pups, ultimately taking to the road with five dogs in a motorhome.

Love, Fluff & Chasing Butterflies is a collection of uplifting, insightful and honest poems inspired by their experiences together.

Presented alongside stylised, incredibly cute images of the furry family as they grow, bond and visit some of Europe's most beautiful scenery, it is a moving collection of verse certain to remind you of why dogs are said to be our 'best friends'.

Find out more at **www.estheranddan.com** or on Amazon.

dog poems inspired by an amazing true story

love, fluff & chasing butterflies

DAN COLEGATE

66820885R00039